CLOSER LOOK AT

THE GREENHOUSE EFFECT

Alex Edmonds

COPPER BEECH BOOKS
Brookfield, Connecticut

© Aladdin Books Ltd 1996
© U.S. text 1997
Designed and produced by
Aladdin Books Ltd
28 Percy Street
London W1P 0LD

*First published in the United States
in 1997 by*
Copper Beech Books,
an imprint of
The Millbrook Press
2 Old New Milford Road
Brookfield, Connecticut 06804

Editor
Selina Wood

Designer
Gary Edgar-Hyde

Front cover illustration
Gary Edgar-Hyde

Illustrators
Ian Thompson
David Burroughs
Ron Hayward Associates
Aziz Khan and Creative Land
Peter Harper
Mike Saunders
Simon Tegg
Peter Kesteven
George Thompson
Ian Moores

Certain illustrations have appeared in
previous books produced by Aladdin Books

Printed in Belgium

Library of Congress Cataloging-in-Publication Data
Edmonds, Alex.
The greenhouse effect / Alex Edmonds; illustrated by Mike Saunders,
Aziz Khan, Ron Hayward associates.
p. cm. -- (Closer look at)
Includes index.
Summary: Presents an overview of the greenhouse effect and its
consequences, explains global warming, and profiles major pollutants
and the damage they cause.
ISBN 0-7613-0545-9 (lib. bdg.)
1. Greenhouse effect, Atmospheric--Juvenile literature. 2. Global
warming--Juvenile literature. [1. Greenhouse effect, Atmospheric. 2.
Global warming.] I. Saunders, Mike, ill. II. Khan, Aziz, ill. III. Ron
Hayward Associates. IV. Title. V. Series: Closer look at (Brookfield,
Conn.).
QC912.3.E36 1997   97-8238
363.738'74--dc21   CIP AC
5 4 3 2 1

CONTENTS

INTRODUCTION

For millions of years the greenhouse effect has kept the Earth at the right temperature to maintain life. Now, because carbon dioxide (CO_2) and other gases released into the atmosphere by people are increasing the "greenhouse effect," some scientists say that the Earth's climate is warming. Nobody is certain about the consequences of "global warming," but if greenhouse gases are increasingly released, the results could be serious for our environment.

W ater, air, and warmth are all necessary for life to thrive on Earth. Although the climate across our world varies dramatically, from the frozen Arctic to the sweltering deserts, the temperature all over the Earth is suitable for different plants and animals to adapt to and survive in.

LIFE ON

Life elsewhere?

The discovery of tiny fossilized bacteria on a meteorite from Mars may point to the existence of life in our solar system. Life can only exist if a planet is not too hot or too cold. On Earth it is the greenhouse effect that creates warmth for life.

All wrapped up

Millions of years ago, before life began, there were more heat-creating gases in the Earth's atmosphere (below) than there are now. If there were as many of these gases now, the Earth would be too hot for most forms of life.

THE ATMOSPHERE

The Earth's atmosphere is a blanket of gases over 300 miles deep. Over billions of years of natural reactions, such as volcanic eruptions, the mixture of gases in the atmosphere has evolved. The lowest layer of the atmosphere, the troposphere, contains the air we breathe and gases that capture warmth on Earth.

50 mi

30 mi

7 mi – the troposphere. Weather occurs here.

Life on Earth relies on energy radiated from the sun, known as solar radiation. The sun's rays are vital as they provide us with heat and light, but if too much radiation reaches Earth it can be harmful.

EARTH

THE SOLAR SYSTEM

None of the nine planets in the solar system have the right conditions for life except Earth. The Earth's average temperature is 57° F (14° C), which can sustain life. On Venus, where there are more gases heating the planet, it is far too hot (an amazing 896° F (480° C)) for life to survive. It is so hot that any water there would boil away. On Mars, where there are fewer gases, it is too cold for life (a freezing -76° F (-60° C)), and the air is too thin to support life.

The Earth is warmed by the greenhouse effect. Naturally occuring greenhouse gases keep the Earth 91.4° F (33° C) warmer than it would otherwise be. The warming effect, in its normal state, is a good thing. But as we send more of these gases that create the greenhouse effect into the atmosphere (through the burning of fossil fuels and the rainforests), the effect increases.

THE GREEN

A glass house
Why is it called the greenhouse effect? Certain gases act like greenhouse glass. They allow the sun's heat into the atmosphere, but prevent a lot of it from radiating back to space.

GREENHOUSE EFFECT

Greenhouse gases allow short-wave radiation from the sun to pass through the atmosphere, but trap some of the long-wave radiation, which is reflected back from the Earth's surface. The greenhouse effect occurs when some of the sun's energy, on being reflected back from Earth, is trapped in the atmosphere by water vapor and a number of other gases, including CO_2.

Atmosphere

Trapped heat

Why do we continue to risk disrupting the climate if climate changes can have drastic effects on life? The dinosaurs died out 65 million years ago due to a major natural change on the planet – possibly a climate change.

HOUSE EFFECT

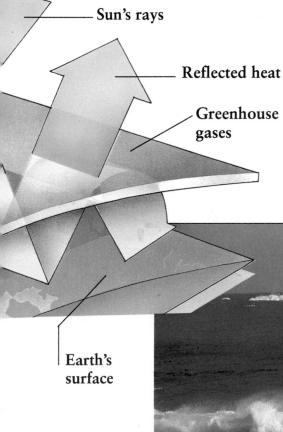

Sun's rays

Reflected heat

Greenhouse gases

Earth's surface

CO₂ IN BALANCE

CO₂, the main greenhouse gas, is kept in balance in the atmosphere by several natural sources. The oceans (below), the atmosphere, and all living things act as both sources and sinks of carbon dioxide. Animals act as carbon sources – they release CO₂ when they breathe and when their remains rot. Plants act as carbon sinks, because they take in CO₂ to grow. Oceans also absorb CO₂. As long as there is a balance between carbon sinks and sources, the amount of CO₂ in the atmosphere will remain the same.

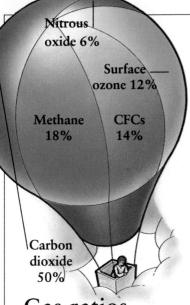

Nitrous
oxide 6%

Surface
ozone 12%

Methane
18%

CFCs
14%

Carbon
dioxide
50%

Gas ratios

*The amount of each of
the five main greenhouse
gases in the atmosphere
(shown above) depends
on how fast each gas is
produced and how
long it stays in the
atmosphere.*

The atmosphere is made up of nitrogen (78%), oxygen (21%), and 1% other gases. Greenhouse gases make up less than 1% of the atmosphere, but they all add to the greenhouse effect. A few artificial substances used in industry, such as chlorofluorocarbons (CFCs), also act as greenhouse gases.

GREENHOUSE

Heat from the
sun warms
the Earth.

Some of the heat
escapes back to
space.

CO_2 is produced by
factories, cars, and
power stations. Cars
also release other heat-
trapping nitrous oxides.

WATER VAPOR

Water vapor is the invisible gas that water turns to when it is heated. It is responsible for about two thirds of the natural greenhouse effect. When water vapor cools, it becomes liquid water droplets, which we see as clouds (above).

ON CLOSER INSPECTION – *Ozone*

Ozone forms 12% of greenhouse gases in the lower atmosphere. In the upper atmosphere it forms the ozone layer, which protects the Earth from UV-B rays. The discovery of a "hole" (right) in this layer has caused people to worry about more UV-B rays reaching us.

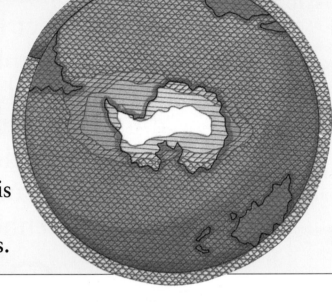

GASES

Methane
Methane occurs in rice paddies and waste dumps, and is produced by cattle when they digest food. It is 30 times stronger than CO_2 as a greenhouse gas but is present in smaller amounts.

Some heat from the Earth is trapped by greenhouse gases.

Methane is an explosive gas produced by rotting waste.

CFCs are greenhouse gases. They can leak from old refrigerators, air conditioners, and aerosols.

Ozone also traps heat.

INDUSTRIAL POLLUTANTS

The world's temperature is about 1° F (0.5° C) higher than in 1860, when measurements were first recorded. This could be due to increased levels of human-made greenhouse gases. These gases are produced by power stations, cars, and factories. As the world's population and industrial activity have increased, so too have the amounts of CO_2, methane, CFCs in the atmosphere, surface ozone, and nitrous oxide. We must reduce these gases to prevent the overwarming of the Earth.

For millions of years, the greenhouse effect has been stable because the amount of CO_2 in the atmosphere has remained constant. CO_2 is the most abundant of the greenhouse gases. Due to human-made pollution it now accounts for more than half of any increased greenhouse effect.

CONCERN

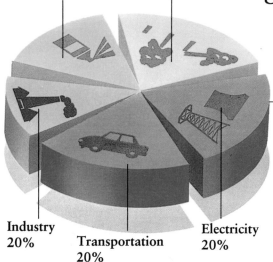

Residential 20%   Deforestation 20%

Industry 20%   Transportation 20%   Electricity 20%

RAINFORESTS AND CO_2

A major concern and source of CO_2 is the burning of the rainforests (right) to make way for agriculture. Rainforest plants, like other plants, take up CO_2 from the atmosphere and turn it into substances that are vital for growth and life. When the trees are burned, the CO_2 is released into the atmosphere. As these trees are destroyed they are no longer there to absorb CO_2 from the atmosphere, so the effect is even greater!

ON CLOSER INSPECTION
– *Natural CO₂*

Volcanic activity also affects climate. Volcanoes produce CO_2 and other gases, such as sulfur dioxide, when they erupt. The naturally produced CO_2 adds to the increased greenhouse effect.

ABOUT CO₂

CO₂ AND TEMPERATURES RISE

This graph shows the average global temperature and CO_2 levels between 1850 and 1990. The blue curve shows CO_2 rises in parts per million (ppm is the way of measuring greenhouse gases), and the red curve shows the rise in average global temperatures. This indicates that temperatures rise as CO_2 increases.

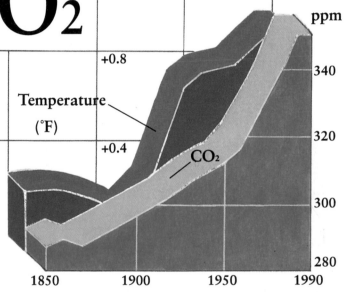

CO₂ culprits

Industrialized western Europe and the U.S. have always produced far more CO₂ than developing nations. But some developing countries, such as China and India, hope to put their huge supplies of poor quality, polluting coal to use. If these large countries do this, the amount of CO₂ emissions would be enormous.

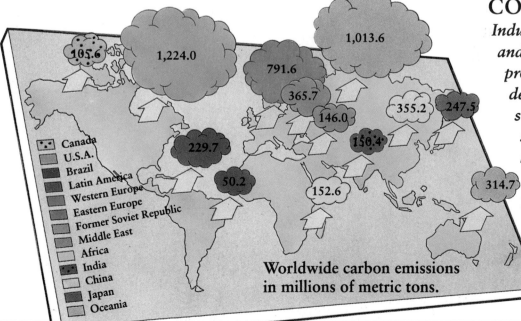

Canada
U.S.A.
Brazil
Latin America
Western Europe
Eastern Europe
Former Soviet Republic
Middle East
Africa
India
China
Japan
Oceania

Worldwide carbon emissions in millions of metric tons.

Pest problems
If the Earth's climate warms up, certain pests are likely to thrive. This could mean that the malaria-carrying mosquito could multiply and spread to northern countries.

Climate normally changes only slightly in a human's lifetime, but can alter dramatically over centuries. Climate change due to global warming is expected to be more sudden, and unpredictable, but no one is certain that it will even happen.

CLIMATE FOR

WHAT COULD HAPPEN

Although the problem is called global warming, it would not simply make the world a warmer place. Some scientists predict huge changes in climate that would have unknown effects on temperature and rainfall across the globe. Some areas of semi-desert may experience more frequent or severe droughts (right). Other colder regions, such as Siberia (far right), could become a farming area if the frozen ground thaws and becomes fertile. This thawed water would also cause floods and destroy buildings.

ON CLOSER INSPECTION
– *Why climate matters*

Climate helps to distinguish one habitat from another. A habitat is the home of a particular group of plants and animals. They depend on a healthy habitat for survival.

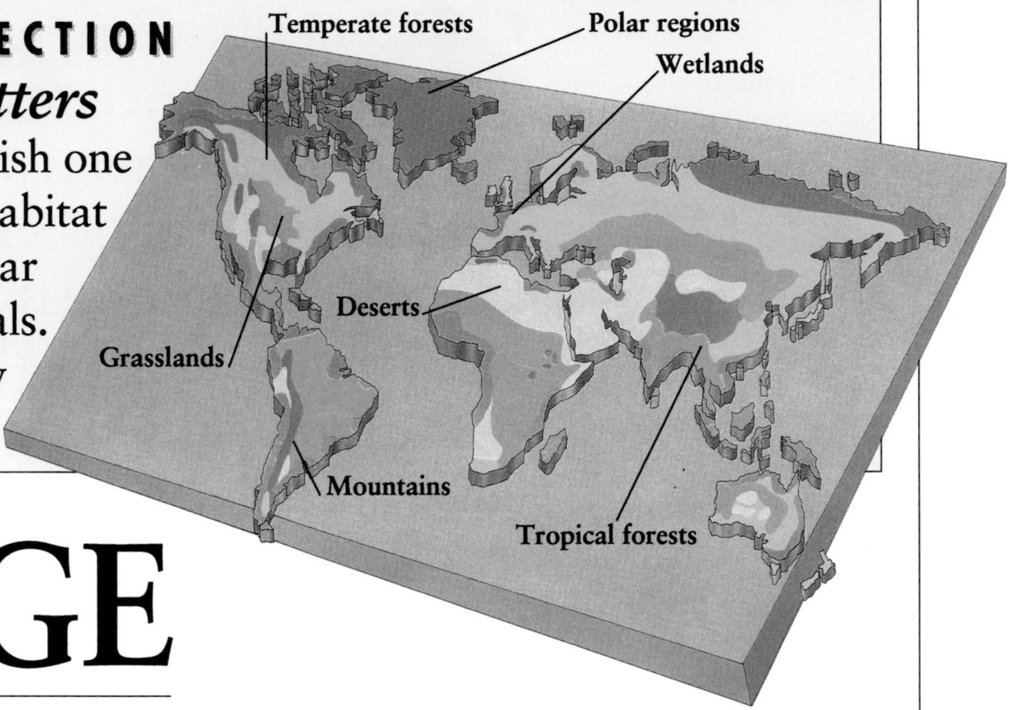

Temperate forests

Polar regions

Wetlands

Deserts

Grasslands

Mountains

Tropical forests

CHANGE

Extinctions

Climate changes have a great effect on wildlife. It is thought that the hairy mammoth died out when a climate change altered vegetation, which made it impossible for it to find food.

Drought
Since 1990 there have been many severe droughts in southern Africa (below). Some scientists believe that this could be part of a natural 20-year cycle rather than global warming.

The six warmest years on record so far occurred in the 1980s. Some scientists believe that these heat waves and other recent cases of extreme weather (such as floods and hurricanes) may be the result of climate disruption caused by global warming.

EXTREME

WEATHER ALERT!

In the U.S. in the late 1980s there were several hurricanes, such as Hurricane Hugo that left 50,000 people homeless. In 1991 many thousands of Bangladeshis died and 10,000,000 had their homes destroyed as a result of cyclone-induced flooding (left). 1992 saw the most tornadoes recorded in the U.S. (11,381). In 1995 the Yangtze River in China flooded (right) due to extreme thawing of snow falls in the Qughai Tibet plateau. These may be due to natural changes in weather, but some scientists say that global warming has begun!

ON CLOSER INSPECTION
– *Wave height*
In the North Atlantic Ocean there has been a significant increase in the average wave height – the size has increased by 25% to 50% since the 1960s. Does this mean that the climate is changing?

WEATHER

Bang! Crash!
In 1987 near-hurricane-force winds in Great Britain caused much damage. By 1992 Britain had had five years of unusually severe storms. Records show that freak weather

conditions worldwide have increased since the 1960s.

Jacksonville

Fort Walton Beach

Tampa

St. Petersburg

Present day

13-26 ft rise in sea level

Miami

Florida at risk

If sea levels increased by 13-26 ft (4-8 m) (over several hundred years), entire cities could be put under water. Florida would be at risk because it is situated on low-lying land (above).

S cientists are certain that if global warming occurs, glaciers on mountains and ice caps in the North and South Poles could begin to melt. Sea levels would then rise, which would flood low-lying land, causing enormous destruction.

FLOOD

Area of Earth's surface covered by winter ice

Area of Earth's surface covered by summer ice

ICE COVER

If the world's ice caps melted, huge quantities of water would be released into the seas; about 99% of the world's freshwater is locked into the ice sheets of Antarctica and Greenland. Vast amounts of methane trapped under Arctic ice would also be released, adding to the greenhouse effect.

ON CLOSER INSPECTION
– *The Netherlands*
Over one third of the Netherlands is below sea level. Dykes have been built to reclaim land from the sea. Other low-lying countries may need to build dams if sea levels rise.

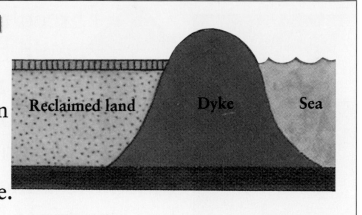

Reclaimed land   Dyke   Sea

ALERT!

RISING SEA LEVELS
Sea levels are already rising by an average of 0.04-0.08 inches each year. If the greenhouse effect (below) increases and causes global warming, the rise in sea levels is predicted to be between 8 and 20 inches by 2050.

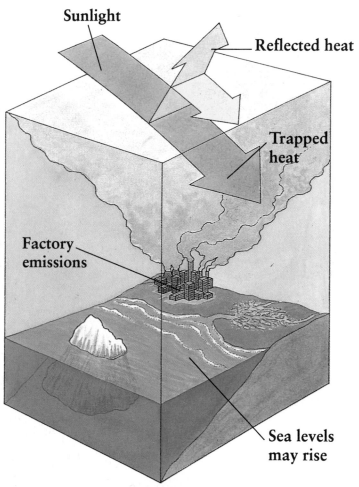

Sunlight

Reflected heat

Trapped heat

Factory emissions

Sea levels may rise

THE MALDIVES
In 1992 the islanders of Nilandu Atoll, in the Maldives, were forced to leave the island due to rising sea levels. Some regard this as some of the strongest evidence for global warming.

If greenhouse gases doubled, there could be a global warming of, 34.7° F to 40.1° F. Once climate is affected by global warming, so too are wildlife, the environment, and people, in much the same way that one falling domino knocks over a line of upright dominoes.

THE DOMINO

Wheat belts

U.S. wheat crops have been badly affected by drought already – since the 1988 heatwave, crop productions are down. This doesn't just affect the U.S.; many developing countries depend on food

produced in the U.S. But there might be a positive side to global warming: In the Northern Hemisphere, crop production may increase because of longer growing seasons.

On Closer Inspection
– Whales

If global warming heated up the oceans, it would affect tiny sea plants called plankton. If plankton were destroyed in the Antarctic, the lives of the whales that feed on them would also be threatened.

EFFECT

FORESTS ON THE MOVE

A rapid change in climate, which might occur through global warming, would force plants to adapt quickly, or die. Some plants can migrate, or move slowly, to climates they can adapt to by spreading their seeds. Not all species can. Most forests disperse seeds to migrate at a rate of a half mile a century (left).

FUTURE PROBLEMS?

Some of the victims of the domino effect could well be people from the poorest areas of the world. Drought or floods caused by global warming could affect water supplies and destroy crops in developing countries such as the Sudan (above right). A recent study from the Worldwide Fund for Nature looked at how China would be affected by global warming (above left). It predicted a reduction in rice and wheat production.

CO₂ levels
This climate physicist is looking at a graph showing increased atmospheric CO₂ levels. The graph is called a Keeling curve.

cientific weather observations have been recorded for 100 years and are used to establish weather patterns. From these records, scientists have been able to tell that the average global temperature has risen by about 32.9° F (0.5° C) in the last 100 years. They are still looking for firm evidence to decide whether global warming is a real threat.

IS THERE

Carbon dioxide in Hawaii
CO₂ levels are tracked at this atmospheric monitoring station (below) built on a volcanic mountain in Hawaii. The location is ideal since it is far away from sources of industrial pollution. Results have shown that CO₂ levels have risen steadily every year.

RECENT RESEARCH
In 1995 a group of scientists explained why the world had not warmed up as much as they had predicted. They suggested that acid rain had had a cooling effect on the climate. They also said that since the 1991 eruption of Mount Pinatubo in the Philippines (above), dust in the atmosphere had been cooling the planet.

ON CLOSER INSPECTION
– *Tree rings*

Tree trunk rings show a tree's growth rate, which depends on weather conditions. These rings can indicate changes in weather patterns, and thus signs of global warming. In Tasmania, tree ring studies show temperatures have risen in the last 25 years.

ANY PROOF?

Estimated future increase of global temperature

On the up!

The diagram on the left shows the average temperature increase since the year 1800. The thermometer on the right shows scientists' predictions of temperature increases in the future, to the end of the next century. It also shows figures as far back as 18,000 years ago. The difference of only a few degrees may seem very little, but it can have a great effect on the Earth's climate.

The greenhouse effect was first discovered by a physicist named John Tyndall, in 1863. Later, in the 1890s, Arrhenius, a scientist, noticed the problems associated with a build-up of CO_2 in the atmosphere caused by burning fossil fuels. It was in the 1960s that the term "greenhouse effect" was first used.

Car crazy

Car numbers are increasing. In Great Britain alone, traffic is expected to double by the year 2005.

THE STORY

Rain

Clouds form

Winds blow clouds toward land

Water seepage

Water returns to seas in rivers

Sea

Evaporation

FINDING THE CULPRITS

In the late 1920s a scientist by the name of Callendar pointed out that between 1890 and then, 150 million tons of CO_2 had been pumped into the atmosphere from fossil fuel burning.

IDENTIFYING THE CAUSES

In 1863, Tyndall showed the importance of water vapor as a greenhouse gas. It forms due to evaporation in the water cycle (above). If the world warmed up, there would be more evaporation and therefore more water vapor, so it would add to the greenhouse effect!

On Closer Inspection
– The good old days?

Earlier this century the city of London, England, was affected by smog, a combination of smoke, poisonous gases, and unusual weather conditions. In the 1950s, the British government made people change to smokeless fuels in parts of Britain.

8565315

SO FAR...

Since then scientists have analyzed the effect of CO_2 build-up in the air, and politicians have resolved to burn fewer fossil fuels.

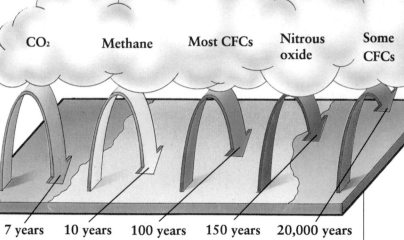

CO₂	Methane	Most CFCs	Nitrous oxide	Some CFCs
7 years	10 years	100 years	150 years	20,000 years

How long will it last?

This diagram shows how long various greenhouse gases stay in the atmosphere. We can see how long-term the effects are. CFCs can remain in the atmosphere for over a century, and up to 20,000 years! This means that we must stop putting more greenhouse gases in the atmosphere now to prevent greater damage in the future.

Air schemes
In badly polluted areas such as Los Angeles, California, air management schemes have been introduced to monitor air quality. Air is sucked in through filters and analyzed for harmful gases.

nternational action is essential to head off the potential problem of the increased greenhouse effect. The first international talks took place at the United Nations Conference on Environment and Development in June, 1992. Its aim is to stabilize the amount of greenhouse gases in the atmosphere at agreed "safe" levels, and to fund further research into climate change and its effects.

THE GLOBAL

UNITED NATIONS
In 1995, at a U.N. meeting on climate change, over 160 countries agreed to begin cuts in emissions of greenhouse gases. In 1997, they will meet again to agree on the targets for reducing these

Forest sinks
A global plan for keeping CO_2 in balance in the atmosphere may include planting more forests. Plantations could act as carbon-sinks to help moderate global warming. They could also provide timber and become an alternative timber source to the valuable rainforests (left).

The cars, factories, and power stations that send CO_2 into the atmosphere are also creating pollution in our cities. This erodes stonework on historic buildings. The Acropolis in Athens, as well as other important monuments (right), is slowly being eroded by harmful emissions.

BATTLE

gases. The aim is to return CO_2 and other greenhouse gas emissions to 1990 levels by the year 2000. The U.N. is also helping developing countries control greenhouse gas emissions.

ED NATIONS CONFERENCE O
RONMENT AND DEVELOPMEN
de Janeiro 3 – 14 June 1992

CATALYTIC CONVERTER

Governments are aiming to reduce CO_2 emissions from transportation. They want to develop energy-saving cars and pollution-free fuels. The catalytic converter – a chamber attached to a car's exhaust system – converts the fumes from exhaust emissions into less harmful substances and is legally required in many countries. Unleaded gasoline also reduces lead pollution.

Cleaner emissions given off

Layers of catalytic chemicals

Filter box

Exhaust gases from engine

Key

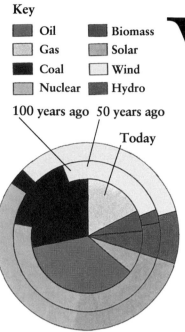

- Oil
- Gas
- Coal
- Nuclear
- Biomass
- Solar
- Wind
- Hydro

100 years ago   50 years ago

Today

W e have been gradually using up the world's energy resources ever since humans discovered fire. Our future depends on our ability to look for alternative energy sources – ones which can be replaced and do not pollute the environment.

AN ALTERNA

What is left?

From this chart you can see that fossil fuels provide for most of our energy needs today. The chart also shows the resources we could use in the future.

Nuclear power

The problem with this energy source is the potential hazard from radioactive waste formed during production.

Solar power – these panels convert the sun's energy into electricity.

Wind power – wind turns the blades of the turbines that drive generators (they are noisy).

Organic fertilizers – are not harmful to the environment. Biomass – methane gas produced from crop waste and animal dung can be used for heating and local electricity generation.

Cleaner cars – unleaded gasoline and catalytic converters reduce harmful emissions from cars.

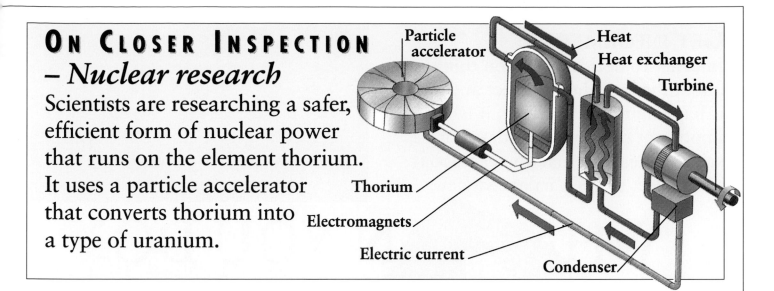

ON CLOSER INSPECTION – *Nuclear research*

Scientists are researching a safer, efficient form of nuclear power that runs on the element thorium. It uses a particle accelerator that converts thorium into a type of uranium.

Labels: Particle accelerator · Heat · Heat exchanger · Turbine · Thorium · Electromagnets · Electric current · Condenser

TIVE FUTURE

Solar power stations – these use solar energy on a large scale.

Public transportation – use of public transportation would reduce the number of cars on the road.

Concept 1

This energy-saving Volkswagen car can be fitted with three different types of engine: The first engine cuts out power when it isn't needed; the second has an electric engine; the third has both electric and diesel engines.

CLEAN ENERGY

To reduce pollution, cleaner forms of energy production must be found and the amount of energy used must be reduced. The illustration above shows some of the ways in which this can be done.

GET INFORMED

In order to decide what you think about the greenhouse effect and what is happening to the world, it is important to keep up-to-date with science. Read all that you can about the subject to get a balanced view.

WHAT CAN YOU DO?

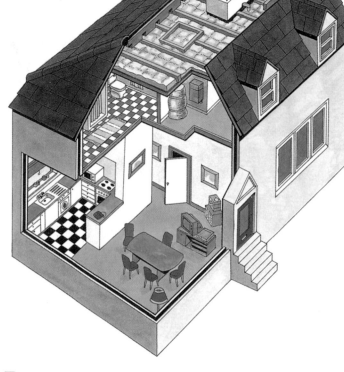

IN THE HOME

We use energy in the home for heating, lighting, cooking, and cleaning. In a home that saves energy, the attic would be insulated, the windows double glazed, and the hot water tank would be wrapped. Perhaps in the future every home will be energy efficient?

PUBLIC TRANSPORTATION

There are more and more vehicles on the world's roads. If more people used public transportation or bicycles, the energy saved would be enormous, and humans would be fitter!

TO SUM IT ALL UP...

The greenhouse effect is an important part of the Earth's natural balance, so we must learn how to avoid disrupting it. We should look toward using renewable energy sources for the future – ones that work in harmony with the Earth, not against it.

GLOSSARY

Atmosphere The layer of gases that surrounds the Earth. It contains the gases oxygen, nitrogen, carbon dioxide, and water vapor.

Atoll A string of coral islands or circular coral reef.

Atom The smallest particle of an element. Atoms combine to form molecules.

Carbon dioxide (CO_2) A colorless, odorless gas. Along with water vapor, one of the main greenhouse gases in the atmosphere.

Catalytic Using a catalyst (a substance that speeds up a chemical reaction).

Deforestation The logging and burning of forests, which has destroyed trees and thousands of animal, bird, and insect species.

Evaporation The process by which a liquid is changed to a vapor.

Extinction When a plant or animal species dies out completely.

Fossil fuel A fuel such as coal, natural gas, or oil, which is formed over millions of years from decaying plants and animals.

Generator A device to turn mechanical energy into electrical energy.

Global warming A gradual increase in temperatures across the world, possibly caused by more heat being trapped in the atmosphere by greenhouse gases.

Greenhouse effect The warming effect created when the sun's heat is reflected back from the Earth's surface and trapped by certain gases in the atmosphere.

Greenhouse gas A gas in the atmosphere that contributes to the greenhouse effect.

Neutron An uncharged particle within the nucleus of an atom.

Particle A tiny piece of matter.

Photosynthesis The method plants use to convert the sun's energy into sugars for growth.

Physicist A specialist in physics (the science of matter and energy and their interactions).

Plankton Tiny plants and animals living on and just below the surface of the sea.

Pollution Contamination of the land, air, or sea with poisonous or harmful substances.

Radiation A way of transferring energy in straight lines.

Solar system The sun, and the nine planets, including the Earth and various other bodies, that orbit around the sun.

Troposphere The lowest level of the Earth's atmosphere that contains the air that we breathe.

Turbine A machine with rotating blades that converts the energy from a moving liquid or gas into another form of energy, such as electricity.

INDEX